The Prayerful Pursuit

75 PRAYERS FOR THE
UNMARRIED MAN

Sam McManus

Gal 3:26-27

ISBN 978-1-7364031-0-5

Edited by Sam Kelly.

Printed in the United States of America.

Cover Design by 100Covers.com
Interior Design by FormattedBooks.com

"Well, just pray about it." How many times have you heard that before in your life? I know I've heard that piece of advice at least a hundred times in the last few years. It's what people often tell me when I'm faced with uncertainty about the future and I'm not sure what God may be up to in the current moment.

As a Christian growing up, I always knew prayer was an integral part in a personal walk with Christ, but to me it seemed like a duty I needed to get done each day. Pray before a meal. Pray before a road trip. Pray before a football game. The list goes on. For most of my life, prayer was something on the list I needed to check off before doing what I actually wanted to do.

It might be like that for you too. Maybe you pray because you were trained to growing up, but you don't really see the point. Maybe you used to pray, but you've recently stopped. Or perhaps you pray frequently because you know it actually works.

Committing my life to Jesus is the best decision I have ever made, and one of my favorite parts about being in a relationship with Christ is how *being* with Jesus comes before *doing* for Jesus. If you know me, you know I am always moving, checking things off my list, and going from one place to the next. I am a doer, and my first instinct is to do. But even though getting things done may allow me to feel more productive, Jesus wants me to begin by being with him rather than by doing stuff for him. If I can get the "being" right, then the "doing" will fall into place. I am thankful for a God who does not evaluate me according to what I get done but rather by the fact that I am made new in my sonship through his Son, Jesus Christ.

So if being with God is the first priority in a relationship with Jesus, how do you actually live out that "being" instead of "doing"? Being with God might look slightly different for everyone, but there is one simple habit that you'll observe in everyone who starts with *being*. By God's grace, this habit allows you, over time, to become a holier version of yourself, and it allows you to meet the right people, allows the right doors to be opened and the right ones to be closed, and brings joy when you need it most. It has the potential to help you leave a godly legacy in your family and influence more people than you ever imagined you could.

Prayer is that habit. Being with God in prayer has the potential to lastingly and radically change your life and the lives of countless others through your influence.

I have written this prayer guide for single men who hope to spend their unmarried years pursuing what matters most. But whether you are a single guy right now or are anyone else in any other life season, being with God in sincere, honest, and vulnerable prayer will profoundly change your life. Whether you are working through your past, trying to figure out your present, or wanting to have a meaningful future, you can attain anything through prayer.

Let's look into the reasons why prayer is important and how you can begin to pray radical prayers for the future.

1. You Are Commanded to Pray

It's natural to question why we should pray to God when, after all, God is the one controlling the universe and not us. How can the prayers I am throwing up to God possibly have an impact on the way the future unfolds?

One of the first realities we must acknowledge concerning prayer is that in Scripture we are commanded to pray. Romans 12:12 tells us to be "joyful in hope, patient in affliction, *faithful in prayer*"; and 1 Thessalonians tells us to "rejoice always, *pray continually*, give thanks in all circumstances; for this is God's will for you in Christ Jesus."

Scripture everywhere communicates to us that we should pray, bringing God our requests. When you think about what Scripture commands, don't forget about the commandment to pray. But even though remembering this commandment might lead you to actually begin praying, it might still leave you with the question "Why does God command us to pray?"

2. Prayer Tests Your Faith

God uses his commandments to test your faith. If you read Scripture, you'll quickly notice that God has always been in the business of testing the integrity and strength of his children's faith. God saw that Abraham had great faith when He asked Abraham to sacrifice his own son. God tested Jesus' obedience in faith when Jesus was tempted in the desert by Satan. Jesus tested Peter's faith by commanding him to step out on water and walk toward him.

God conducts these tests by giving you commands and watching to see if you obey them. The command to pray is one that God uses to reveal whether you indeed trust him. God calls on you to pray so that he can see the quality of your faith.

3. Prayer Unlocks God's Plan

The great German theologian Martin Luther once said, "Prayer is not overcoming God's reluctance. It is laying hold of His willingness." When you pray, you are not giving God a new idea of what He can do, nor are you changing God's plans. Instead, God invites you into a relationship with him through prayer so that you can play a part in unlocking the plan God has for the world. As beings made by God, we have the opportunity to bring about what God has planned through our very obedience. As humans we cannot change the heart of God, but we can discover his heart through our time with Him in prayer.

Minneapolis pastor John Piper has said, "God plans our prayers just as surely as he plans the events that he performs in answer to our prayers." God knows the prayers you are going to pray, and those prayers serve as stepping-stones to the unfolding and unlocking of the future. Often, we can trace the events happening in our lives as answers to the prayers we prayed in a previous season.

4. Prayer Anchors Your Relationship with God

One of my favorite characteristics of God is that you can always trust that there is purpose behind anything he commands. Sometimes you can see that purpose clearly, but often the purpose is hidden, challenging you to trust in

God's sovereignty and allowing God to reveal it according to his timing. With the prayers that God asks you to pray, he has layers of concealed purposes that you might only begin to notice over the span of your lifetime.

If you step back and begin to think about it, why should a God who is all-knowing, all-powerful, and forever existent command the prayers of finite, imperfect, mortal human beings? The answer to this question lies within the very nature and character of God. Because of the love God has for each of us as his own creation, he longs to have a very personal connection with us. God doesn't sit in heaven with his arms crossed, laughing at the desperation of humanity; instead, he asks us to present our requests and our needs to him. God wants to be in an intimate relationship with you.

Spending time with God in prayer anchors you in the relationship God wants to have with you. If you take a second and think about a meaningful relationship you have with someone else, I'm willing to bet this relationship has great meaning to you because of the time you have spent with that person. In order to build a relationship with God, you must spend time with Him, and God has made prayer to be a place where that relationship can grow and develop. So, as you think about what it might look like to step into a habitual prayer life, imagine how deep your relationship with God can grow.

Prayer also fosters the essential trust that is needed in a relationship with God. In John 10, Jesus calls us his sheep and calls himself the Good Shepherd. Sheep must trust their shepherd to lead them to places where there is abundant grass to eat and where they can be safe from predators. We can also trust Jesus as our Shepherd. However, unlike sheep, we are invited into a conversation with our Shepherd, and through that conversation we have the opportunity to build our trust that Jesus will lead us to the pastures we need to be in.

Furthermore, prayer shows us how dependent on God we really are. Sheep are incredibly dependent animals and rely heavily on their shepherds for survival. Some sheep will actually die without a shepherd to care for them. They are vulnerable to predators, and without shearing their wool can overgrow, causing them to overheat or impeding their mobility. Sheep depend on a caretaker, and we too can't go very long without our Good Shepherd leading and caring for us. Prayer is constant communication and lets God know how dependent we are on him.

Finally, prayer constantly reminds you of and anchors you to your identity in Jesus. When your identity is rooted in Christ, you have a solid foundation on which you can live your day-to-day life. I know I have struggled to remember the liberating truth that I am operating from Christ's victory and not trying to attain it. Just think about it: How often do thoughts cross your mind that discourage you, demotivate you, or deceive you? You cannot win this daily battle in your mind yourself, and when you pray, you invite God onto the battlefield and retreat back onto the solid foundation of Jesus. Through prayer, God counters the lies you are tempted to believe, and he anchors you to the identity he has bought for you with Christ's blood.

As you begin to get closer to your Creator, your prayers will become more intimate and personal. You'll begin to let God into what is really on your heart, and in turn he can do the real work that needs to be done inside of you. Praying wild, unordinary prayers over your own life and your future is one of the best habits you can develop, and it will lead you to a more godly and faithful life.

As you embark on this prayer journey, know that there is nothing inappropriate about reading scripted prayers that someone else has already written. Beginning to pray with a guide is a great way to take the first step toward building an intimate relationship between you and God. Scripted prayers can serve your prayer life like a runway serves an airplane. You don't want to stay there forever, but using them at the beginning of your journey can propel you to a more whole-hearted relationship with God. That why this book contains only seventy-five prayers, because I hope it will launch you into a powerful prayer life that is uniquely yours and God's.

Additionally, you'll notice that this book is called a prayer guide rather than a devotional. That's intentional. As you become familiar with this book and begin to see how it fits into your prayer life, you might choose to pray one of these prayers each day, you might choose to pray a handful of them in a day, or you might come back to them occasionally as you feel the need. Be sure to note the date you prayed each one so that, down the road, if you notice an answered prayer, you can celebrate God's faithfulness to your requests.

The prayers in this book fall into three categories. First, the majority of this journey focuses on praying for your life right now, because if you don't love, know, and grow yourself, it's much harder to teach and lead others to do the same. (In this book, this first type of prayer is distinguished by ⛰ at the top of each page.) The second category (distinguished by ⛰) focuses on praying over your future wife right now, and the third (distinguished by ⛰) focuses on praying over the marriage you will share. So, there are "me," "she," and "we" prayers.

And as you pray these three kinds of prayers, you must remember to do three things.

Ask for Wisdom

Even though most people who are reading this book will be in a similar season of a life, you have unique circumstances and need individual guidance based on where you find yourself right now. I want to encourage you to ask for wisdom from the Holy Spirit as you begin this journey. Ask him to show you when to pray these prayers and when to spend time with him in another way. Ask him to show you when to pray for yourself and when to pray for your wife or your future with her. Scripture tells us there is a time for everything (Ecclesiastes 3:1), and God is gracious enough to make those seasons clear to you through the Holy Spirit if you ask.

Steward, Don't Idolize

One of the biggest reasons you should pray for this wisdom is that, without it, you might come to idolize a particular area of your life. Praying over your future wife, family, and goals is necessary, but if you aren't careful, you can begin to make too much of particular hopes for your future and use prayer as merely a means to an end. Remind yourself that the goal of your prayers is not to fix everything that is wrong in your life or to give you your dream life in the future. Focusing only on the outcomes could lead you to miss out on the abundance of lessons God needs to teach you right now during your single years. If you notice yourself becoming infatuated or consumed with a particular prayer point, pivot and pray over something else. Additionally, as the Lord guides you in his perfect wisdom, don't be afraid to take a break from reading these guided prayers and resume this journey when you're ready. Remember, there is a time for everything.

Act Faithfully

Recently, I noticed myself becoming more anxious in situations where I had never experienced anxiety before. When I began to take an inventory of myself, hoping to get to the root of this anxiety, I noticed I was praying a lot but that my prayers were not succeeded by any action. I asked the Lord to bless conversations, Bible studies, and my work, but when I began to feel insecure and discouraged about them, I turned to prayer again without following through with action, and in turn I began to doubt that God could actually sustain me and answer my prayers. I kept praying and praying, and before long, I drove myself miserable because I felt that God was ignoring what I asked him to do.

Every year, a time comes when farmers begin to plant seeds in the ground with the anticipation of reaping an abundant harvest months later. Farmers have no idea when rain will come to water and nurture their crops, but they choose to plant seeds anyway and trust God though faith that He will provide the rain. Our prayer life needs to function the same way. We must put our faith into action and humbly expect and anticipate that God is going to do something with the prayers we have planted. We cannot sit inside all day hoping and praying for rain and choose to plant only when we see the water falling; instead we must go into the field and prepare and plant seeds and expect the rain we know God is bringing.

Though my prayers were centered on the Lord's good will, I was failing to actually display my trust in God through my actions. After a friend encouraged me to do so, I decided to trust that I was equipped to participate in conversations, engage in a Bible study, and do my job, and I stepped into action and felt the anxiety begin to melt away. As you pray these prayers, do not let your waiting become passive, and remember to accompany your prayers with action.

As you seek out new ways to pray over your current and future life though this exciting prayer journey, please know that I will be keeping you in my prayers.

Dear Lord, I thank you for the man who has picked up this book and has decided to pursue you through prayer over his present and his future life. I pray that you bless this man, that you make your presence known in his life today, and that you guide him in your wisdom so that he may pray over the areas in his life you want him to pray over at the right times. Father, give him the shield of faith to protect him from the flaming arrows of the evil one, and let him renounce in Jesus' name the lies coming from Satan. Let him be a man after your own heart—obeying your commands, not chasing the gold and silver of the world—and let him find faithful brothers in his corner to walk the journey of faith with him. Father, may these prayers bear fruit in your perfect timing, and may you allow him to learn from his suffering, grow in his pain, and live in the victory of your Son. I pray that you would remind him constantly of the identity that he has been given through the death and resurrection of your Son. Amen.

1

A Solid Foundation

"So neither the one who plants nor the one who waters is anything, but only God, who makes things grow. . . . By the grace God has given me, I laid a foundation as a wise builder, and someone else is building on it. But each one should build with care. For no one can lay any foundation other than the one already laid, which is Jesus Christ."
1 Corinthians 3:7, 10–11

A house is only as stable as its foundation. The foundation of your life is Jesus Christ, and when you build on Him, you build a life that can stand through life's toughest storms. Ask God that you may have the desire to begin building your life on what really matters.

Lord, thank you for the opportunity I have to come to you in prayer and make my requests known to you. I praise you that I do not have to build my own foundation but that I can build my life on the foundation that is already laid in Jesus Christ. I pray that you guide me and help me to build on your foundation with care. Show me what is wise, make clear to me what is holy, and reveal to me how to build with integrity so that I may stand firm through life's storms. Help me to find the space to be with you and hear from you, and help me to maintain the desire to speak to you. Allow me to plant seeds now that will produce a harvest of righteousness, and shape me into the man you want me to be. Help me to go all in on this journey with you. Amen.

2

Seeking Wisdom

"Blessed are those who find wisdom, those who gain understanding, for she is more profitable than silver and yields better returns than gold."
Proverbs 3:13–14

Wisdom is the attribute that will help you tell a good decision from a bad one and will help you choose between multiple good options when you must. Pray that God would give you wisdom generously so that you can make decisions that please him.

You are great, you are powerful, you are holy, and you alone are worthy of praise, Jesus. Thank you for accepting my praise to you today. Today, I come before you to ask for just one thing, but it is one thing that can radically change my life. I ask you, God, for wisdom—not the kind of knowledge that yields pride, but a portion of your holy and all-knowing wisdom. Lord, please instill within me your holy and righteous understanding, knowledge, and counsel so that I may have a peace that surpasses all understanding. Every day, I will make choices, many of which will have a lasting effect on my life and the lives of others; so God, I ask for you to give me unending wisdom so that I may make choices you will be pleased with. Help me to be a man who craves wisdom and who is after your heart. Amen.

3

A Friend of God

"You adulterous people, don't you know that friendship with the world means enmity against God? Therefore, anyone who chooses to be a friend of the world becomes an enemy of God."
James 4:4

Often, it's easier to compromise God's commandments and to submit to what the world demands of you. Pray that you may secure your marriage under God and not become a friend of the world.

Dear God, thank you for your trustworthiness—that I can follow you without hesitation or doubt and without having to question your character. I pray today that I may not be a friend to the world and that I may constantly turn my gaze to my eternal home with you. Let me see the things of this world as reflections of your beauty and also as an opportunity for your redemptive power to be displayed. Let my wife and I do this throughout our marriage and throughout the days when we lead our family; help us to focus on pleasing you and honoring your kingdom rather than becoming friends with the world. Give us courage to do this, Lord, when the world is against us and no one is for us. Help us to maintain our eternal perspective. Amen.

4

Practicing Hospitality

*"Share with the Lord's people who are
in need. Practice hospitality."*
Romans 12:13

Scripture highlights and honors the men and women who practiced hospitality toward those in need. Pray that you can display hospitality to those God puts on your path.

Father, I come before you this day to thank you for the new seasons of life that are to come one day, and I want to pray over the season of marriage that is to come. I ask that my wife and I may be a lighthouse in the darkness for the community we live in and an encouragement to the body of believers we belong to. Let us, Father, share the resources you give us with others, and show us, Father, who needs the blessing we can provide. Let our house serve as a safe harbor for those in difficulty so that we may point people to the one who gives all of us grace. Let my wife and I demonstrate hospitality within the walls of our home to missionaries from afar and to our neighbors next door so that Christ may be magnified. God, please dwell within the walls of our home and make your presence known there. Amen.

Finding Freedom

"It is for freedom that Christ has set us free. Stand firm, then, and do not let yourselves be burdened again by a yoke of slavery."
Galatians 5:1

You have to clean the mud off your glasses before you can keep walking forward. Singleness affords time to work through past struggles and wounds, allowing you to reflect the power and work of Christ. Pray that God would begin to reveal to you where you need find freedom in your life.

Lord, thank you for never leaving your children and for staying close to us every day. Lord, you know what kinds of hurts are in my heart, and you know what I have been through in my past and how that is affecting me today. I pray that I may use this time to find freedom from my past so that I am not carrying these burdens into my future. Thank you for being present during this process. Help me to find the right people to confess my hurts to, and allow me to find healing in community. Reveal to me the root causes of my struggles so that I may eliminate my hurts at the root and not only on the surface. Cast out any anxiety from within me in your name, and allow me to be *vulnerable and honest with others. I know this may be a pain-ful journey to embark on, but I also know that finding healing in Jesus' name was never meant to be safe and that it is always worth it in the long run. Thank you for the freedom I can find in your Son's name. Amen.*

Loving Next Door

**"Each of us should please our neighbors
for their good, to build them up."**
Romans 15:2

Jesus frequently taught that you should love your neighbors. Taking this commandment literally, pray for opportunities to love the neighbors near whom you and your wife will one day live.

God, I am grateful for the gifts you have given me, the purpose you have instilled within me, and the opportunities I have to make a difference in this world. I pray that my wife and I may make a difference in the lives of the people who live near us geographically once we are married. Father, let us love our next door neighbors, our neighbors to the left and the right, behind and in front. And to the people we call our neighbors in the community we involve ourselves in, God, let us be your hands and feet to make a spiritual difference in their lives. Bring into our lives neighbors who have needs so that we may bless them and serve them on your behalf. Show us the needs of our neighbors and equip us with your love so that we may bless our neighbors for your kingdom and reflect the love Jesus has shown us. Amen.

7

Facing Pride

"I am the vine; you are the branches. If you remain in me and I in you, you will bear much fruit; apart from me you can do nothing."
John 15:5

Pride kills. It tells you that you can do things on your own and causes you to build your own kingdom instead of God's kingdom. Pride will block you from growing, learning, and believing the truth about your identity. Today, ask God to reveal the pride in your life.

Dear Lord, I thank you for the plans you have and for allowing me to be a part of your story. Lord, can you show me where I have pride in my life? I come before you to ask that you may wash away any hints of pride that are growing inside of me. Jesus, you were the ultimate picture of humility, and I desire to be humble like you. Let me constantly be learning and never be wise by my own standards. Remind me that there is no good I can do without you. Humble me, because my pride creates a barrier between me and you. It stops me from truly experiencing the love you have for me and your wisdom. Take me from the reliance I have on myself to a complete dependence on you. Let me not put confidence in my own works but in the mighty things your name can do. Amen.

8

Fear of the Lord

"Charm is deceptive, and beauty is fleeting; but a woman who fears the Lord is to be praised."
Proverbs 31:30

The woman you may marry one day is out there living her life right now. Because you put your hope in God, you know that, even if you don't see it, you can trust he is working. Spend some time praying over your wife's day today, and ask God to shape her into a God-fearing woman.

God, I come before you to ask for blessings today for the woman I will one day be able to serve alongside as a husband. I pray that this very day, throughout everything she might put her mind to, that she puts you first. Let her pray before making her decisions, and let her have a thirst to be one with you in an intimate relationship. For the hardships that will come, I pray that she may trust you boldly and persevere so that her character is refined. Let her have faith that your perfect plan and will is unfolding in her life even if she doesn't see it. Let today's events, people, and thoughts lead her right back to you. I pray that she may be encouraged by those who love her most and that you put others around her to speak your truth to her. Amen.

Overcoming Shame

"As Scripture says, "Anyone who believes in
him will never be put to shame.'"
Romans 10:11

Often, shame can creep into your life without you even noticing it. God doesn't want you to live in shame because it creates a barrier between you and him, preventing you from experiencing his love. Pray that you may recognize any shame in your life and cast it out in Jesus's name.

God, I thank you for the purposes you have for my life and how I can trust your leadership every day. I thank you for the cross and the drastic debts you chose to pay in my place. I thank you that because of Christ's death and resurrection, I will never be put to shame and you have afforded me a life of freedom during my time on earth. I pray that when I fall short of your glory and when I sin, I do not cycle into shame and become stuck in the patterns of toxicity that Satan will attempt to trap me in. Instead, I pray that your Holy Spirit would convict me and lead me to rejoicing in your freedom. Jesus, help me to see a clear picture of your freedom every day and approach you with a clear view of grace.

Your Inner Circle

"Jesus took Peter, James and John with him and led them
up a high mountain, where they were all alone."
Mark 9:2

Every man of God needs brothers to walk alongside. Jesus was close to Peter, James, and John and found support from these men. Pray that you may find an inner circle of brotherhood in your life too.

Father, I enter into your presence today as a family member to thank you for adopting me and bringing me into your house. I am grateful for the believers you have surrounded me with in my daily life, and I praise you for the lessons the people around me can teach me. I pray that I can follow the example of your Son by having an inner circle of brothers so that I may be sharpened. I pray that you will provide me with my own Peter, James, and John and that I can find accountability from, encouragement from, and unity with men who are also your disciples. Allow me to say no to the wrong people and yes to the right people. Father show me this grace in the present and in the variety of seasons that are to come in my life.

11

Life as a Single

"The disciples said to him, 'If such is the case of a man with his wife, it is better not to marry.' But he said to them, 'Not everyone can receive this saying, but only those to whom it is given.' "
Matthew 19:10–11 (ESV)

Jesus tells us that some people are called to a life of singleness. Spend some time asking the Lord to show you if you might be called to such a life. Whether you remain single for a few more months, or for life, pray today that you may be anxious to go after God's heart.

Dear Lord, thank you for loving us with grace and truth. Today, I come before you to ask, if I am called to a life of singleness, that I may use my life to be a faithful servant to your kingdom. I know that being called to such a life allows me not to be more available to myself but more available to you and that there will be countless opportunities for me to serve your name. I pray that you would sustain me, provide for me, and nurture me as a single man so that I may live freely and with contentment, with a mindset that is calibrated to usefulness as a member of your family. Guide me to the communities you need me to serve and lead me to new groups on your timing. I pray that I may find true joy and fulfillment by pursuing your heart. Amen.

12

Humility in Marriage

"Then Jesus said to his disciples, 'Whoever wants to be my disciple must deny themselves and take up their cross and follow me.' "
Matthew 16:24

Following Christ requires humility and sacrifice of one's self. Marriage works in the same way: you must deny yourself, seeking the honor of your spouse. Pray today that you aren't seeking marriage to fix your issues and that you will rather seek to humbly sacrifice for your wife.

God, thank you for the relationship I will one day have with my wife. I pray that in my marriage I will honor my wife with humble sacrifice and commitment to her. I pray that I will honor her above myself and seek her flourishing. I pray that I will constantly be reminded of my desperation and need for your power that is made available through the cross. Let me not trick myself into believing that once I am married, my temptations will melt away and my bride and I will live together perfectly forever. Father, I pray pride will not creep in and tempt me and my wife to become independent from each other and from your saving grace. Give us the audacity to be honest and the ability to be patient with each other in our trials and temptations. Let us each pick up our cross daily to follow you, now and in marriage. Amen.

Spirit over Soul

"The mind governed by the flesh is death, but the mind governed by the Spirit is life and peace."
Romans 8:6

Your soul—that is, your mind, will, and emotions—is vulnerable to sin, but God says his Spirit is stronger and is willing to help. When your mind, will, and emotions begin to conform to the patterns of the world, invite the Spirit to govern them.

God, I come before you with a heart of thanksgiving for the miracle of life I am experiencing today. Today, I seek you purposely for the supernatural part of me: my spirit. Lord, will you continue to make your home within my spirit and connect my spirit to your Spirit? I pray fervently for amplification of the Spirit in my life so that he may govern my soul. I ask you, Father, that my mind, will, and emotions will align and be congruent to your Spirit. May your Spirit govern my mind and block out the sinful thoughts that try to take root in my head. The mind of a sinful man is death, but a mind controlled by the Spirit is life and peace. I pray that the Spirit would be the one in control even when my emotions are running high. Thank you for giving us insight to your power. Amen.

14

Spirit over Body

"But if Christ is in you, then even though your body is subject to death because of sin, the Spirit gives life because of righteousness. And if the Spirit of him who raised Jesus from the dead is living in you, he who raised Christ from the dead will also give life to your mortal bodies because of his Spirit who lives in you."
Romans 8:10–11

Your physical human body naturally desires sin, and sin ultimately leads to death. When you are tempted to indulge your fleshly desires, God says you can invite the Spirit to overcome your temptations. Pray that you would allow the Spirt to call the shots in your life.

Heavenly Father, thank you that you chose to design us humans in the likeness of your very being. Thank you that my spirit connects to your Holy Spirit and that your Spirit has the power and authority to prevail over my soul and my body. Today, I ask you, God, that your Spirit would govern my body. I know that my mortal body is dead without the Holy Spirit and that it naturally craves the desires of this lost and broken world. Holy Spirit, I pray that you will govern my mind so powerfully so that my sinful patterns of lust, debauchery, and addiction may be eradicated in Jesus's name. Let me live a life centered not on satisfying the desires of the flesh but on satisfying your desires. Spirit, align my body with your compelling and effective power. Amen.

Biblical Finances

"A good person leaves an inheritance for their children's children, but a sinner's wealth is stored up for the righteous."
Proverbs 13:22

God takes delight when you manage your finances well. In the United States, financial issues are a leading contributor to division in marriage. Pray you and your wife may be unified under God when it comes to money.

God thank you for using money to bring us closer to people through business and through giving, and thank you for using it to test our faith through our stewardship of what you have provided. I pray today that my wife and I may be powerfully united when it comes to how to manage our finances. Let us be good managers of the money you have given us. Help us to provide for the necessities of our household and of your household, the church, first. Then help us to invest in our future, for our retirement and college for our children. Help us to leave an inheritance for our children and our children's children. Then allow us to go into the world and serve our local community and the greater world for your kingdom. Thank you for trusting us with your money; let us be good stewards and do the little things well. Amen.

Humanity Tested

"The Devil, playing on his hunger, gave the first test:
'Since you're God's Son, command this stone
to turn into a loaf of bread.' "
Luke 4:3 (MSG)

In the wilderness, Satan tempted Jesus to act on what his flesh desired. Satan will often tempt you to indulge your humanity, telling you to satisfy yourself with something of the world. Pray that you will rely on Jesus to help you overcome Satan's temptations.

Jesus, thank you for choosing to come down to this planet and acquaint yourself with humanity. God, thank you for allowing your Son to face temptation and prove to Satan the victory that resides in heaven. Jesus, thank you for allowing your faithfulness to be tested in the desert. I know I will be tempted to give into the desires of my flesh daily, and I pray that I will cling to the truth that the gold and possessions of the world are not worth disobeying you. My flesh is a gift from you, but through sin it is weak. Father, help me to honor my body as a living sacrifice to you always, and let Satan not win me over through his temptations. Help me to not seek after the bread of the world but to seek the bread of everlasting life. God, thank you for the power you give me. Amen.

17

Identity Tested

**"Then the devil took him to the holy city and had him
stand on the highest point of the temple. 'If you are
the Son of God,' he said, 'throw yourself down.' "**
Matthew 4:5–6

"If you are . . ." When Jesus was in the wilderness facing
temptation from Satan, his identity was targeted twice (see
Matthew 4:2–3). Satan will attack your identity today. Arm
yourself and pray that you may stay rooted in what is true
about you.

*God, thank you for the story of your Son and for giving your children
like me hope through the defeat of Satan. Jesus, your identity was
tested multiple times when you were tempted in the desert. Father, I
pray that today and every day for the rest of my time on this planet
that I may realign to the identity you have paid for me to live in.
Satan is in the business of attacking our identity, and he will not
stop attacked mine. I say out loud today that I am a son of God,
and a child of the King, I am holy and dearly loved, and I am*

bought with a price. Satan has no power over my identity. God, provide me a way out when I face the temptation to forget my identity, and give me people to remind me of that identity today and forever. Thank you, Lord, for calling me yours. Amen.

18

Loyalty Tested

"Again, the devil took him to a very high mountain and showed him all the kingdoms of the world and their splendor. 'All this I will give you,' he said, 'if you will bow down and worship me.' "
Matthew 4:8–9

Jesus's loyalty was also tested during his time in the wilderness. Pray that you may remain loyal to God even when you find yourself in a wilderness season with the Lord.

Jesus, thank you for the ways in which you defeat Satan daily. Thank you for the story of your Son defeating the evil one. I pray I may do the same through your holy power. God, your Son's loyalty to you was tested by Satan in the desert, and I know that in the same way Satan tempted your Son, he is coming after me. Father, I pray today that I can be loyal to you. Let me cling to you always, and help me to not lust after another leader, ruler, power, or authority. Your governance is sovereign and whole and far more powerful than anything I can fathom. Jesus, I want to be loyal to your Word, your commands, your Spirit, your promises, and your leadership of the church. Let me never dedicate my loyalty to anyone or anything else. Amen.

Him First

**"Commit to the Lord whatever you do, and
he will establish your plans."**
Proverbs 16:3

Everything we do is a picture of the grace and mercy of God. The very act of living is a miracle, and we can praise our God for that. Pray that you may commit everything you do to Him first.

Jesus, I thank you for your endless mercy in my life. I pray your will would be done on earth as it is in heaven. Jesus, thank you for the opportunities that are to come in my future. I come to you in a posture of worship now to ask that you allow me to commit to you everything I may do in the remaining days of my life. Before I begin a new project, before I begin a school assignment, before I enter into a new relationship, before I have a child, I pray that I have the courage to commit whatever and whoever to you. My life is not my own, and it does me no good to pretend it is, so today and for all the days going forward, I commit to you everything I put my hands to. I love you Lord. Amen.

A Generous Wife

*"When it snows, she has no fear for her household; for
all of them are clothed in scarlet. She opens her arms
to the poor and extends her hands to the needy."*
Proverbs 31:20–21

Pray that your wife will be a woman who is happy to follow
the Lord's calling and a woman who takes delight in help-
ing those in need without demanding anything in return.

*Dear Father, thank you for creating me, for creating my future wife,
and for giving both of us skills and talents that we can use to mag-
nify your kingdom. I ask that she would take delight in taking care
of our household and that she would be proactive in serving our
children. Let her show agape love and promote the flourishing of
each individual she encounters. I pray that I would make space
for her to open our house to the poor and to the needy and that I
am inspired by how she cares for and serves others. Thank you for
the influence she can have on people throughout her lifetime, and I
pray that I would empower her to love and bless as many people as
possible. Thank you for describing what a woman after your own
heart looks like in Scripture and for honoring such women. Amen.*

Following God

**"Instead, you ought to say, 'If it is the Lord's
will, we will live and do this or that.' "**
James 4:15

God sometimes keeps our plans from coming to pass to make sure we really do trust him. Pray today that you may submit to the plans that God has for your life and that you will be available to go where he calls you.

God, thank you for the chance I have in this world to have a career, earn a living, make decisions, and plan for what is ahead. Thank you that I have the chance to pray over my future life, my future spouse, and my future family. Thank you that I can bring this request to you and that you are overjoyed to hear requests like this from your son. Let me not attempt to manage my own life without regard for you or mislead myself through my own pride. Thank you for having all my days planned for me even before I was born. Let me present my requests to you daily, but let me also say, "If it is the Lord's will." I am not my own and choose to follow, submit to, and enjoy the leadership of the Good Shepherd leading me to the fields I need to be in. Your will be done in my life. Amen.

22

My Identity

**"The Spirit you received does not make you slaves, so that you
live in fear again; rather, the Spirit you received brought about
your adoption to sonship. And by him we cry, 'Abba, Father.' "**
Romans 8:15

Being a son of God is the pinnacle of your identity as a
man. Though you don't deserve it, God has chosen to
adopt you into his family. Step into your sonship today
and remind yourself of the truth that never changes.

*God, I pray that today I may live according to my true identity.
Guard me from the temptation to try to earn it. I know my identity
is already bought and established through the blood of your Son,
so today I choose to operate from that truth and know that I am
always your son. Let me not attempt to work for your love but to
soak in it. Thank you for making me holy and blameless in your eyes
despite my past and present sin. I don't deserve the grace by which
I have been adopted into the family of the King, so I thank you for
it. Thank you for pursuing me and for choosing me as a member of
your family forever. Please help me to do the works you need me to
do for your kingdom. God, have your way today. Amen.*

23

Pursuing Peace

*"Blessed are the peacemakers, for they
shall be called sons of God."*
Matthew 5:9

You and your wife will undoubtedly face challenges in your life. Pray that God may use you as peacemakers to reflect God's character among others.

Dear Lord, I thank you for your help in the desperate areas of my life and the grace you show me even when I do not realize it. Father, I know I might get married one day, and so now I come before you to make my requests known to you as I approach this potential season in my future. I pray that you bless my marriage with love, compassion, and generosity and that it would be rooted in your truth. I pray that through these fruits we may live at peace with everyone. I pray that our marriage would be an icon of peace in the environments that we find ourselves in so that we may show your character of peace through our actions. Let us live at peace with those we come in contact with, be they our family, church groups, neighbors, or coworkers. Show us how and where to have boundaries with others who do not promote peace. Let us live at peace with everyone. Amen.

24

A Graceful Life

"See to it that no one falls short of the grace of God and that no bitter root grows up to cause trouble and defile many."
Hebrews 12:15

Your life is a testament to God's heart of grace. Pray that you can show the heart of your Father through your actions today.

Lord, thank you for your consistency with your love. No matter how many times I come short, you continue to love me and pursue me with your fierce love. I pray that I would give the most generous gift I can today: grace toward others. Even when it is hard, even when they don't deserve it, even when the person I need to extend grace to has wronged me sevenfold, let me demonstrate your grace. Let me show grace that is genuine, grace that loves through actions and through words, and grace that is kind. Allow me to pray for others, especially those who have wronged me. Help me to learn more of the ways you extend your holy and unending grace to all people, Father, so that I may do the same too. Amen.

Pursuing Wisdom

*"Be very careful, then, how you live—not as unwise
but as wise, making the most of every opportunity,
because the days are evil. Therefore do not be foolish,
but understand what the Lord's will is."*
Ephesians 5:15–17

God's wisdom is one of the keys to authentic and sustainable joy in your life. Wisdom guides you on the path of the Lord and allows you to become confident as you trust God. Ask the Lord for His wisdom to take over in your life.

Jesus, thank you for the gift of the Holy Spirit, whom you have given to your people. Lord, even though the world will tell me otherwise, I pray that I would recognize that the wisdom of your Holy Spirit is one of the most precious gifts I can receive. I ask that you would grant me wisdom for my future. I ask you for the type of wisdom that does not come from the scholars of this world but from the voices of heaven. I pray that you would grant me wisdom that yields purity in my life, values peace, seeks compassion, honors submission, pursues mercy, and desires obedience. Show me how to make the most of every opportunity, and show me where to draw boundaries. As a tree is judged by the fruit it produces, I long to produce the good fruit of your wisdom within me. Instill within me your sincere and complete wisdom that is made available only through your power. Amen.

Seeking the Spirit

"For the Spirit God gave us does not make us timid,
but gives us power, love and self-discipline."
2 Timothy 1:7

We aren't capable of overcoming the challenges of this world without God's power. Pray that your future spouse may experience the Spirit's power, love, and self-discipline in her life today.

God, thank you for using people to communicate your story. I pray you are writing your story on the life of my future wife today. Let her experience your Spirit today through your word and through your people so that she may feel your power, discipline, and love. Infuse her with power and allow her have victory over her temptations today. Lead her in discipline today as she goes about her routine. May she not forget to include you in each step of her day. Bring love into her life today and allow her to love herself and in turn love those she comes in contact with. Let people see Jesus through this woman. God, thank you for her. Be with her today and protect her. Amen.

Hope in Trials

"We also glory in our sufferings, because we know that suffering produces perseverance; perseverance, character; and character, hope. And hope does not put us to shame, because God's love has been poured out into our hearts through the Holy Spirit, who has been given to us."
Romans 5:3–5

Paul tells us in Romans that suffering leads to something better. First, suffering leads us to perseverance, then character, and eventually it pushes us to hope. Pray that you and your future wife will find great hope in the midst of your sufferings.

Dear Heavenly Father, I thank you for the confidence of the future that I can focus on today. I thank you for the hope of what is ahead not only during this earthy life but also in heaven and on the new earth. I ask you, God, that when I am married, when my wife and I face difficulties and hardships, that we may keep our eyes centered on the love and hope of your sovereignty. Let us faithfully reframe our approach toward the difficulties we face so that we may not be disappointed in the long run. I pray for perseverance in the challenges that together we may work to endure the hardships on this fallen earth and that in turn we may gain stronger and more steadfast character in the grand scheme of our life together. Amen.

28

Healthy Anger

**"A hot-tempered person stirs up conflict, but
the one who is patient calms a quarrel."**
Proverbs 15:18

Becoming angry is not a sin, but you can sin when you
become angry. As issues arise, pray that you may have
patience and that the anger you experience will not lead
you into sin but will rather help you grow.

*God, thank you for your work in my life and the provision you have
made from the day I was formed in my mother's womb until the
day I leave the earth. God, I come before you to make yet another
request known to you. I pray this verse over my week, month, and
the future seasons that, if you will it, I am to experience. Please give
me a heart of patience so that I may calm the storms and quarrels
I walk into in the future. Let me not sin against you when I am
angry. I pray that you would highlight any areas of my life in which
I am harboring anger and nourishing a hot-tempered spirit within
me. Guide me in a life filled with your patience so that I may show
your steadfast love to others. Amen.*

Parenting

"Start children off on the way they should go, and even when they are old they will not turn from it."
Proverbs 22:6

Being a parent is one of the most rewarding things you will do in life, and it has the potential to pull you closer to God in new ways. Pray that God would be at the center of your parenting.

God, thank you for the opportunity we have to love others, and specifically to love the children that you may bless us with one day. Though I don't know when I'll enter the season of fatherhood, I come before you now to ask for your hand to be on my family's future generations. God, I pray against any fear that might begin to build up as we approach this new season, and I pray for confidence in Jesus's name and that we may step out in faith into this season of parenting. I ask that you place wise counsel around us to teach us your principles, your discipline, and your wisdom. Let your Word be the backbone for every action and lesson we give to our children, and let us grow in new ways in our relationship with you during parenthood. Let us not set a standard of perfection for ourselves, but let us rather point our children back to the one who is perfect and to the one who does have all the answers.

30

Seeking Truth

"Stand firm then, with the belt of truth buckled around your waist, with the breastplate of righteousness in place."
Ephesians 6:14

If God is truth, then to reject truth is to reject God. Pray that you might seek God's truth revealed in his Word and not settle for any counterfeit.

God, thank you for the ability to know and understand. Thank you that I can discover the truth and that I am not seeking to create it. Thank you that I have the ability to know what is good and to know what is true and beautiful. God, I pray to you now that I would root my life in your unwavering truth and that I would not give into the lies that Satan presents to me daily. Let me not stray from your ultimate truth as I take in knowledge from the world. I pray that I can operate from your truth just as Jesus did, that I may be able to speak, believe, preach, teach, and live out the truth of Scripture. Let me meditate only on what is true and what is pleasing to you, and let my character be rooted in nothing short of your truth as I become more like Jesus. Amen.

God's Blessing

*"The Lord bless you and keep you; the Lord make his
face shine on you and be gracious to you; the Lord
turn his face toward you and give you peace."*
Numbers 6:24–26

A prayer of blessing is a way of asking for God's divine provision. The Lord gave Moses this simple prayer of blessing
that his brother, Aaron, the high priest, could speak over the
Israelites. Ask for God's blessing for your future marriage.

*Father, you are welcome into this place today as I pray this prayer. I
praise you for your willingness to always meet me where I am. I pray
for your favor and protection for the marriage I may enter into one day.
I pray that you would be pleased with the commitment my wife and I
make to each other and that you would get the glory and the honor. I
pray for your grace and your mercy during all of our days together and
that we may humbly accept your protection. I pray for your righteous
peace throughout the days of our marriage and that your Spirit would
rest on us and provide us with the power we need to do your will and
make a difference on this earth. Thank you so much for your love for
your children and for blessing us with your love. Amen.*

Pursuit: When

*"There is a time for everything, and a season for
every activity under the heavens. . . .
A time to search and a time to give up, a time
to keep and a time to throw away."*
Ecclesiastes 3:1, 6

There is a time for everything, and the right time to pursue a woman is something the Holy Spirit can reveal to you. Pray that He would show you when the time is right to initiate a relationship.

God, I come before you on this day you have made with a humble heart that is grateful for your plans and provision for my life. God, I want to ask for your wisdom about the timeline of the pursuit of a girl I might one day call my wife. Guide me and communicate to me if you need me to grow right now in my singleness or if the time is right to begin something new. Help me to never feel inadequate or unworthy to pursue someone, and help me to not become prideful as I pursue someone. Jesus, you pursued your church, but you did it on your perfect timing, waiting thirty years before your ministry began on earth. So, I ask for wisdom today on when I should pursue my bride. Thanks for deciding to put me on earth during this specific time in history. I trust you God. Amen.

Pursuit: Where

"This is what the Lord says—your Redeemer, the Holy One of Israel: 'I am the Lord your God, who teaches you what is best for you, who directs you in the way you should go.' "
Isaiah 48:17

God has always been in the business of leading people to the right places so that his grace and his glory will be magnified. Just as God led the Israelites to the Red Sea to display his power there, ask the Lord to lead you to the places he wants you to be.

God, I am grateful for the countless mercies I have experienced thus far today, and I want to make a simple request. I pray that you would provide me with the right church, community, neighborhood, and career to pursue a godly woman and marry here. I pray that I may find myself in the right places to meet someone I could pursue, and I ask that you would guard me from the places of this world that bear no fruit. I pray, when I do begin to pursue her, for spaces and places to do so. I pray that I may have opportunities to pursue her in person and in a place that is accessible to both her community and mine so that we may benefit from their wisdom. Amen.

34

Pursuit: Who

"A wife of noble character who can find? She is worth far more than rubies. Her husband has full confidence in her and lacks nothing of value. She brings him good, not harm, all the days of her life."
Proverbs 31:10–12

There are many women out there whom you might date, but not all of them are people you would be wise to date. Pray that God would show you the right person to date and that you would have the power to say no when you need to.

God, thank you that at the cross you redeemed a people for yourself. Thank you that among those people is one I might one day call my wife. I seek your face this day to ask you to lead me to the woman I should pursue. I pray that I would not become lazy and fall for girls who go after the ways of the world and seek to satisfy the desires of their flesh. Guard me from temptations that only yield short-term satisfaction instead of sustainability. Introduce me to women who have their eyes fixed on you. Keep me focused on you, God, so that at the proper time I will see the "who" of my pursuit. In the places you lead me, I pray for the right faces to meet me. I pray that I may be led to the one you have handpicked for me on your timing.

35

Pursuit: How

"Husbands, love your wives, as Christ loved the
church and gave himself up for her."
Ephesians 5:25

Jesus pursued you by giving himself up for you. For your sake, he centered his whole life on sacrifice. How can you mirror the same sacrificial love and pursue your future wife like Jesus pursued his people, the church?

Father, thank you for pursuing us. Thank you for the loving arms you extend to me and the peace you provide as a Father to your children. Thank you for pursuing your church and for becoming one with your bride. I pray that I can pursue my wife with the same grace, peace, and love you pursued your bride with. Help me to show the heart of pursuit before marriage and during every single day of marriage too. Show me your tactics of pursuit with the always-forgiving heart and the grace that keeps no record of wrongs. Let me always be accepting, and allow me to become one with her just as you became one with the church. Thank you for being bold and for giving us an example to follow. Amen.

36

Forgiveness

"Then Peter came to Jesus and asked, 'Lord, how many times shall I forgive my brother or sister who sins against me? Up to seven times?' Jesus answered, 'I tell you, not seven times, but seventy-seven times.' "
Matthew 18:21–22

Twenty-four hours a day, God chooses to forgive us no matter what sins we commit. How can you show this same grace to your wife one day?

Father, thank you for the opportunity of marriage I might one day have. Thank you for graciously giving me a woman to love, cherish, and serve. I know my wife will not be perfect, and I ask that I do not set that standard for her today. I ask for help showing her relentless forgiveness every single day, just as you show us daily. I pray that as a way of loving her I might listen intentionally to her heart of confession. I pray that I might cherish her and see past her mistakes to gracefully love her as you so fervently love us. Let us find your forgiveness in prayer, and let us not hide behind shame. I pray you would use the mistakes and sins in our lives to make us stronger in your name. Let me serve her more passionately and let us love you more intensely. Amen.

Making Peace

**"If it is possible, as far as it depends on
you, live at peace with everyone."**
Romans 12:18

God delights in peace. Pray today that you would be a catalyst for peace.

Dear Father, thank you for your good works in the lives of the people of this world. I thank you for your goodness and peace that is made available to everyone through your Son. I pray that I may live fully in you and that peace may be a byproduct of my sonship in your name. I pray to you, Father, that I may live at peace with everyone, so long as it is up to me. I pray that I am slow to speak and quick to love and that I do not repay evil for evil. I pray, Lord, that your grace would be at the forefront of my actions, that your patience would guide my every action, and that your love would rest on my lips. I pray that you would give me your wisdom for when to confront, fight, and challenge, and when to turn my other cheek. Father, I pray for a life of peace with others in the days, months, and years to come. Amen.

Loving Yourself to Love Her

"However, each one of you also must love his wife as he loves himself, and the wife must respect her husband."
Ephesians 5:33

Paul tells men to love their wives as they love themselves. If you don't love yourself well, you won't be able to overflow with authentic love for your wife. Pray that you may begin to have a healthy view of yourself so that your marriage will be built on love that lasts.

God, I pray that I may continue to live out of the identity you have paid for me to live in. Thank you for the solid foundation of your Son that I may operate from. I pray that because of the way you see me and because your ways are true, I may love myself and be reminded of the value I have in your family. Unselfishly, I pray this—so that later in my life I may love my wife as I love myself. Let me provide for her as I provide for myself, anticipate her needs as I anticipate my own, value her thoughts as I value my own, honor her as I would want to be honored, and lead her to you, Father. Let my love for her never fail as your love for your bride, the church, goes on forever. Lead me to humility in your name. Amen.

Identity

**"Christ loved the church and gave himself up for her . . . to
present her to himself as a radiant church, without stain or
wrinkle or any other blemish, but holy and blameless."**
Ephesians 5:25, 27

Living consistently out of the identity that God gives us in
Christ is a challenge for everyone. Pray that your future
wife can operate from how Jesus sees her today.

*God, thank you for calling us your own and for calling us by name.
Thank you for showing us your love out of a reflection of your character and thank you that your love does not need to be earned. I
lift up the woman I hope to one day marry, and I pray that she
lives from the identity she has in you. I pray that she would walk
by the truth of this verse so that she might experience daughterhood
from her Father as Christ advocates for her, making her holy and
blameless in his name. Let her feel the weightiness of the peace this
identity entails, and help her to believe she is worthy. She is not
working to become holy but is made holy through your blood, so I
ask that you would give her the capacity to believe that today. Let
her be wrapped in your deep love today. Amen.*

Glory

**"For by him all things were created, in heaven and on earth,
visible and invisible, whether thrones or dominions or rulers or
authorities—all things were created through him and for him.
He is before all things and in him all things are held together."**
Colossians 1:16

Do you ever stop to wonder and marvel over the glory of the God we serve? Take a few minutes today and bathe in the magnificence of our King.

Dear God, I bow down in your court today and fix my eyes upon your glory. I worship your limitlessness and your radiance today and marvel at you for being a God over all the universe. You are the King over the earth, the moon, the galaxy, and everything else in all creation. God, I ask you to make yourself known today where I live. Be here in my house, in my region, on this continent today, God. Bring your presence and make yourself known. I praise you for being the God of all nations and cultures in all the earth. Thank you for your omniscience and for knowing all the details of my life. God, you are worthy, and you alone are to be praised. Thank you that even though you are the most powerful being in all the universe, you are also the most loving, caring, and compassionate. Thank you for choosing to be a good Father to your children. Amen.

41

___ / ___ / ___

Inner Circle

"Do not be yoked together with unbelievers.
For what do righteousness and wickedness have in common?
Or what fellowship can light have with darkness?
What harmony is there between Christ and Belial?
Or what does a believer have in common with an unbeliever?
What agreement is there between the temple of God and idols?"
2 Corinthians 6:14–16

Relationships shape who we are and who we become. Ask the Lord to show you which ones you should be a part of.

Lord, thank you for the opportunity I have to build relationships today. Show me the current relationships I should nourish and the new relationships I should add to my life. Make known to me which relationships yield fruit in my life and which relationships show no fruit. I pray for the relationships with family that I have today that are not whole, that you would reveal to me how to make them whole again. Help me to live at peace with everyone and to find freedom and forgiveness from the damaged relationships of my past. Speak to me through the people around me, and speak through me to the people that need to hear it. You are a relational God, so I choose to make strides in my relationships today. Amen.

Family Unity

"Whoever brings ruin on their family will inherit only
wind, and the fool will be servant to the wise."
Proverbs 11:29

Families can be tricky, and merging your family with your
wife's family will take some intentionality. Pray now for
peace in these new relationships.

Our Father in heaven, hallowed be your name. I come before
you today in an eager posture to praise you and make my
requests known to you. I ask for your guidance over the rela-
tionship between my family and my future wife's family. Only
you know the intricacies of my family and her family, so I ask
now that you would prepare to bond the uniqueness of the two
families together. Let us have boundaries where we need to have
boundaries and let us be bold to establish those boundaries with
both families. Let our family reflect the unity you want to have
with us. I ask that I may live in lifelong harmony with my future
in-laws and treat them with respect, showing the fruit of the

Spirit in my relationships with them. Begin to bond all the broth-
ers, sisters, cousins, aunts, and uncles into one family in your
name. I pray for peace, joy, and healthy intentionality between
all members of our families for all the days we might live. Amen.

Future Generations

"Children's children are the crown of old men,
And the glory of children is their father."
Proverbs 17:6 (NKJV)

There is a good chance of you having your own grandchildren one day, and Scripture says there is much delight to be taken in your future generations. Spend some time in prayer for your children's children today, and ask the Lord to protect and bless them.

Dear Lord, I thank you for the opportunity I have right now to plant seeds through prayer that can be harvested over a lifetime. I come before you today to lift up the children who will be carrying my family legacy in the future. Even though I am not married now and do not have children of my own, I ask that you bless my grandchildren. I pray for God-fearing parents in their lives and that these young boys and girls can have proper models—men and women who are after your heart. I pray for a strong faith to ignite among these children and that the flame is not easily extinguished. I pray for unity among their parents, their siblings, and their cousins so that they may find peace with and love for one another. Let them be hard-working, making a difference in this world, and allow them to remain healthy physically, emotionally, and spiritually. Anchor my grandchildren in your truth, Lord, and protect them from the temptations of this world. Thank you, Lord. Amen.

44

Discipleship

"And whoever does not carry their cross and
follow me cannot be my disciple."
Luke 14:27

Discipleship is spending time with Christ to learn from him and to be more like him. You have the opportunity to be his disciple, so ask him to help you carry your cross daily and live in total submission to him.

God, I am so grateful today to be called your son. Thank you for adopting me into your family and paying the full price for me to live freely in you. I pray that today I would be your disciple. In my quest of discipleship, I pray first that I would spend more time with you in prayer, in your word, and in conversation with your Spirit. Second, I ask that I would learn from you. Teach me your principles and guide me in your truth. I pray that I would acquire more knowledge and wisdom from the stories written about you in Scripture. Finally, I pray that I would become more like you. I pray that through the time I spend with you and the things I learn from you that I would be refined into a man of Christ. Amen.

45

Encouragement

"But encourage one another daily, as long as it is called 'Today,'
so that none of you may be hardened by sin's deceitfulness."
Hebrews 3:13

Everyone who has breath in their lungs right now needs encouragement. Start by praying for encouragement for your future wife today.

Father, hallowed be your name. Thank you for allowing me to offer up these prayers for encouragement for my future wife. Lord, today I pray for our future marriage. I pray that my spouse and I, whoever she may be, may persistently encourage each other. As long as it is called "today," let the two of us turn to each other to spur one another on so that we may continue to run the race with perseverance. When times are smooth and when times are challenging, show us how to keep encouraging each other, and give us your insight into where we each need it most. Let our mutual encouragement guard our hearts from sin. Thank you for encouraging your children through your children. We love you. Amen.

46

Discernment

"Do not conform to the pattern of this world, but be transformed by the renewing of your mind. Then you will be able to test and approve what God's will is—his good, pleasing and perfect will."
Romans 12:2

Discerning God's will can be tricky, and it is probably a challenge for your future wife, too. Pray for discernment in her life today and that she may hear clearly from the Lord.

Dear Heavenly Father, today I ask that my wife may find clarity. Undoubtedly, she will face choices, each with different paths, and each path with different outcomes. So, Holy Spirit, I ask that you would give her the wisdom she needs to walk down the path you want her to be on. God, guide her to the paths that continue to lead to your grand plan for her life. Give her the ability to say yes to the right opportunities and no to what could set her back, and grant her a desire to only set her mind on what is above. Please do not let her conform to thinking of this world or get caught on the hooks and lures of the temptations around her. Be with her today, God—intersect with her in the way only you can. Thank you for watching over her. Amen.

47

Protection from Satan

"And pray that we may be delivered from wicked and evil people, for not everyone has faith. But the Lord is faithful, and he will strengthen you and protect you from the evil one."
2 Thessalonians 3:2–3

You are guaranteed to be attacked by Satan during your life here on earth. The good news is you possess a shield that is stronger than his attacks. Pray that you may rely on the shield of faith given by our God and that you will live in faith that he will protect you.

Thank you, God, for the hedge of protection that you place around your sons and your daughters. I ask you to spare me from the evil one in my time now before marriage. I am weak, and I am a vulnerable sheep in a pasture, but I pray to the Good Shepherd to fight off the roaring lion that tries to attack me. I pray today for your protection throughout each second of today and over all the thoughts that circle in my head. Thank you for your faithfulness and for loving me so much that you want to guard the gate and protect me. Satan has never been, is not, and will never be more powerful than you, so I pray that I will never believe the lie that he is. May your shield defend me from the constant and never-ending arrows Satan fires at me. I choose to walk in faith today that you will protect me. Amen.

48

Grace

"And from his fullness we have all received, grace upon grace."
John 1:16 (ESV)

Even though we don't deserve the grace of God, he shows us grace in many ways. We ought to thank him for it. Thank God today for the grace he will show to you in the future through your wife.

Dear Father, thank you for the gift of your Son to a world that was lost, broken, and in desperate need of saving grace. You have given me the gift of grace freely, without my asking for it, because you loved me so much. Father, I pray that this love you have for me and this passionate relationship between us is manifest in my relationship with my wife. Thank you for giving us reminders of grace daily, and I pray I can be a reminder of grace to my wife. I pray that just as you exemplify true grace, my wife would be a tangible reminder of grace to me every day. I pray that my wife would love me through all of my days. Let her be the consistent voice and picture of your love in my life. Amen.

God's Love

"For I am convinced that neither death nor life, neither angels nor demons, neither the present nor the future, nor any powers, neither height nor depth, nor anything else in all creation, will be able to separate us from the love of God that is in Christ Jesus our Lord."
Romans 8:38–39

Where you sin, how you sin, with whom you sin—none of these can separate you from God's rich love for you. Being aware of his vast love for you can help you eliminate the impurities in your heart. Take some time to soak in his love today.

It is an honor to serve a God like you, Father. Thank you for the abundant provision you've made for your sons and daughters, never abandoning us even for a second. I know your love for me is deep, but the world so often persuades me otherwise, lying to me and saying that your love is hard to find and that is doesn't last. Today, I pray that I would sink into the deep love you have for me. I pray, when the darkest of days come and when I sin against you, that I continue to drown in the perfect love you have for me. Let me not believe the lies of Satan. Instead, let me freely partake in your devoted love for me. Amen.

Fatherhood

**"As a father has compassion on his children, so the
Lord has compassion on those who fear him."**
Psalm 103:13

God is the perfect example of a good father. One day, you
might become a father to children of your own. Pray that
the love your Heavenly Father has for you will overflow
into your love for your children.

*God, thank you for your love and the righteousness you display
to your children around the world. Thank you for exemplifying
fatherhood so well to us. Thank you that I can jump into your
loving arms that are extended toward me and are ready for a whole-
hearted embrace. Thank you for the listening ear you provide for
all the requests I have and for the advice you give from your abundant wisdom. Thank you for the grace you show me every single
day, especially after I do things you have clearly told me not to
do. Thank you for showing me what it means to be creative and
what it means to work and be rewarded for my labor. Thank you*

for the discipline you give me and the people you place around me so that I may grow and develop as your son. I pray I can adopt all these attributes you portray as a father in my role as a father one day. Amen.

51

Seeking Truth

"Everyone has heard about your obedience, so I rejoice because of you; but I want you to be wise about what is good, and innocent about what is evil."
Romans 16:19

Many people in the world will try to lure you away from the truth with attractive lies. Pray today that you and your wife will cling to truth and become wise about what is good.

Thank you, Lord, for your goodness and the opportunity I have to display my devotion to you through prayer. God, I pray that when my wife and I are faced with the lures and hooks of this world, we may seek your truth together that leads to life everlasting. Let us desire to have wisdom about what is good and be innocent toward evil. I pray that you would give us wisdom generously so that we can know the truth that aligns with your character and that we may have nothing to do with smooth talk, flattery, or the ways of this world. Throughout our marriage, let our joy be rooted in your truth, even if your truth is countercultural, and let us crave truth from you only. Thank you for the words you have breathed out to humanity, which we have in the holy Scriptures. Amen.

The Shield of Faith

"In addition to all this, take up the shield of faith, with which you can extinguish all the flaming arrows of the evil one."
Ephesians 6:16

A shield protects you as you charge into battle. Do you believe that your faith can protect you from evil as you charge into action in your life? Pray to live in godly faith today.

God, thank you for giving your children tools to fight against the rulers of this world and the powers of the evil one. Thank you for establishing a beachhead for your victory, which I have the joy of living under. Today, I pray I can take up the shield of faith so that I may focus on your promises, root myself in your power, and enjoy the peace that comes from having a solid foundation in you. The enemy will fire his flaming arrows at me daily, so let me take up my shield of faith and live in confidence that you are sovereign and are stronger than his attacks. Let my faith be expressed in action and obedience in my life. Thank you for allowing me to have hope in the future because of your consistent goodness and power. Amen.

Wisdom

"But the wisdom that comes from heaven is first of all pure; then peace-loving, considerate, submissive, full of mercy and good fruit, impartial and sincere."
James 3:17

Scripture says wisdom is more profitable than silver and yields better returns than gold. Invest in your life now by praying for wisdom for your future.

God, thank you for your willingness to give your children what they need. I pray that in the midst of the chaos in the world I will have wisdom that comes from heaven. I ask you, God, that I would be able to reject living according to the world's way of thinking and seeking solutions and that instead I would accept your wisdom, which is more valuable than my own. I pray for wisdom that yields a desire to create peace in the world and to seek a pure heart. Allow me to have conversations with those whom I disagree with. Show me how to promote peace and forgive the mistakes of others while being genuine with them. Let me show grace while remaining rooted in your truth, and guard me from mistaking my own understanding for your wisdom. Amen.

Shame

"Or do you show contempt for the riches of his kindness, forbearance and patience, not realizing that God's kindness is intended to lead you to repentance?"
Romans 2:4

God is kind no matter what we do, and His kindness continues especially when we sin. In fact, Scripture says kindness convicts us and brings us to our knees in repentance. Pray that you and your wife will also show kindness that leads to repentance.

God, I am grateful to you for allowing me to wake up this morning and for the hours you have graciously given me today. I thank you for your willingness to hear all my requests. Today, I ask that my spouse and I may not experience long-lasting shame in our relationship. I ask, God, that when one of us sins or does something to offend the other, we never feel isolated by the other. Let us instead be drawn toward repentance through the kindness we have for each other. Shame leads us to isolation and separa-

tion, and shame can block us from unity with you. I pray that through the conviction from the Holy Spirit of our wrongdoing that we may both always approach each other with love and with grace. Amen.

God's Approval

"Am I now trying to win the approval of human beings, or of God? Or am I trying to please people? If I were still trying to please people, I would not be a servant of Christ."
Galatians 1:10

It's easy to strive to please the world, but pleasing God is what actually counts, and his acceptance is more fulfilling, consistent, and available. Jesus sought God's approval, not the approval of people, so pray that you will too.

Father, I thank you for the opportunities I have to be a light in this world. I thank you that you give us such thrilling experiences as humans and that I can choose the work that I do, gather with close friends, and partake in my hobbies and interests freely. I pray that through these things I will not seek people's approval. In a world where it is so easy to base our value on comparison to others, I pray you would guide me in finding value in you alone. I pray that I wouldn't live for the approval of others so that I won't die by their disproval. Align me to your acceptance, Jesus. Amen.

Spiritual Gifts

"These members do not all have the same function, so in Christ we, though many, form one body, and each member belongs to all the others. We have different gifts, according to the grace given to each of us."
Romans 12:4-6

Paul writes that everyone has unique gifts that can be used to love and serve others. Pray that you will identity these strengths and steward them well for God's kingdom.

Thank you, Lord, for the unique ways in which I am designed. God, I ask that I may uncover more of my unique design and that I may discover the spiritual gifts that you have given me. I know sin has distorted my view of myself and that it prevents me from knowing the value I have, so allow me to have a healthy appreciation of myself. Father, I ask that you help me believe that I am holy and dearly loved, that I am blameless, that I am a son of God, and that you have bought me through the power of your blood. As I understand how you have created me, I pray that I will honor the gifts you have instilled in others and that I will seek the flourishing of your people. Let me be a sacrifice to others for your kingdom. Amen.

57

Generosity

"Whoever sows sparingly will also reap sparingly, and whoever sows generously will also reap generously. Each of you should give what you have decided in your heart to give, not reluctantly or under compulsion, for God loves a cheerful giver."
2 Corinthians 9:6-7

God loves a cheerful giver. Ask the Lord to help you and your wife become more and more generous toward others as you grow older.

God, thank you that my identity is not found in my money, but in your love. I pray that my future wife and I would be good stewards of what you entrust to us and that we would be good managers of the money you give us. Since everything on this earth is already yours, let us bring to you the money that you already own and give it generously to others. Allow us to support the church and missionary work and meet many other financial needs in the community we live in. Show us where to give and who to give it to, and help us to be good managers of what you have given to us. I pray that if we become more financially stable and blessed, that we would only become more generous. Let us bring to you at least a tenth of what we earn each year. Amen.

Good Fruit

"He cuts off every branch in me that bears no fruit, while every branch that does bear fruit he prunes so that it will be even more fruitful."
John 15:2

Jesus has a mission for your life, and bearing bad fruit only prevents you from carrying that mission out. Pray that God would reveal to you the bad fruit in your life so that it will not keep you from advancing his kingdom.

Jesus, I praise your holy name today and set it above everything in this world. It is worth more than any human mind can fathom. God, make your power visible today, and allow me to produce the fruits of your Spirit as a disciple of Christ. Reveal to me the offenses in my heart that are blocking me from producing life-giving fruits in your name. Show me any action that is doing damage to your name, and convict me of the ways I have turned from you in my disobedience. I pray that those who have not been sanctified by your name would see your good work in me and that I may be a light to the those who are in darkness. Thank you for the opportunity I have to be obedient. Help me to stay rooted in humility, and allow me to be patient with myself as I begin to display your fruits more in my life. Amen.

God's Word

"Keep this Book of the Law always on your lips; meditate on it day and night, so that you may be careful to do everything written in it. Then you will be prosperous and successful. Have I not commanded you? Be strong and courageous. Do not be afraid; do not be discouraged, for the Lord your God will be with you wherever you go."
Joshua 1:8–9

Scripture refers to itself as a sword, an offensive weapon used to get up close and personal with the enemy (Ephesians 6:17). Pray that you and your wife might use the words of truth to fight your battles in the future.

God, I am grateful for a physical record of your grace on earth and its availability in my own language. Thank you for a tangible gift from you and a gift that guides us on the path to freedom in your name. I pray that my future wife and I would not depart from the teachings of your book but rather that we would put your words on our lips and that we recite them day and night. Let every day we live increase our desire to read your word and to store it in our hearts. Spirit, guide us in what we need to read and what we need to mediate on, and engage us in your teachings and grace every day. Create in us a supernatural thirst that can only be quenched by your word. Amen.

Community

"Two are better than one, because they have a good return for their labor: If either of them falls down, one can help the other up. But pity anyone who falls and has no one to help them up. Also, if two lie down together, they will keep warm. But how can one keep warm alone? Though one may be overpowered, two can defend themselves. A cord of three strands is not quickly broken."
Ecclesiastes 4:9–12

Having community is essential to following Christ. Pray you will seek healthy community even when you're married.

God thank you for who you are and for making your power accessible. Thank you for how you speak through people on your behalf and use them to remind me of the grace of your Son. I pray that when I am married, both my wife and I would have healthy community, both individually and as a couple. I pray you would provide me with other Christian men who will keep me accountable, motivated, and encouraged and that I would be a better husband because of the community I have. Let my community call out offenses in my life that don't bring honor to you, and let it constantly point me to the person of Christ. Let my future wife find godly women who push her closer to you and keep her accountable to your word. I pray that she would be a better wife through the community of women surrounding her. I pray this all under your word. Amen.

Love that Lasts

"Love is patient, love is kind. It does not envy,
it does not boast, it is not proud."
1 Corinthians 13:4

The love the world shows and the love that Jesus shows are vastly different. Pray that you would mirror Jesus's love and not fall into the trap of giving unsustainable, worldly love.

Thank you, God, for centering everything around love. You are love, and thank you for overflowing that love so that we may love others. I ask that the love between my future wife and I would be the epitome of your love. I specifically ask today that our love would not be rooted in pride or arrogance but instead in humility, kindness, and patience. Let my wife and I root our love for each other not in our distinctions and accomplishments; rather, let us love each other sacrificially. Let our love be a love that seeks often and serves kindly. I pray that if, in the future, we begin to root our love in something other than Jesus Christ, we would be quickly convicted so that we can find freedom and joy again through the love of your Son alone. Amen.

62

Pursuit

"What do you think? If a man owns a hundred sheep, and one of them wanders away, will he not leave the ninety-nine on the hills and go to look for the one that wandered off?"
Matthew 18:12

We are called to be active, not passive. Jesus showed his activeness when he pursued his church. Pray that you would have the same heart of pursuit that Christ does.

God, I am humbled at the deep love you show your children without ceasing. I thank you, Jesus, for deciding to be one with your bride, the church, and that you chose to pursue us even when we did not choose to pursue you. Thank you being gracious in your pursuit while also demonstrating what it means to be a man in the image of God. I ask that I would have the same heart of pursuit that you do. Jesus, you left the ninety-nine to seek the one, and I want to mirror your heart of bold and loving pursuit. Teach me the way of forgiveness, grace, peace, and sacrificial love that you embody when you pursue us. Help me to spend more time with you so that I, as a son of God, may participate in the great pursuit that you modeled to us so well. Amen.

Identity

"For you created my inmost being; you knit me
together in my mother's womb. I praise you because
I am fearfully and wonderfully made; your works
are wonderful, I know that full well."
Psalm 139:13–14

Your identity is one of the most important things about
you, yet it is often the most insecure. Step into your true
identity in Christ and speak it over yourself constantly.
Pray that you may begin to operate from the truth of who
you are in Christ.

Dear God, today I am eternally grateful for the identity you have
given me. Thanks for knowing who I was before I was born and for
never leaving me during any second here on earth. Remind me of my
sonship in you. Remind me today that I am created in your image
and that I resemble you physically, in my soul, and in my spirit.
God, thank you for allowing me to be holy and dearly loved by you
and that you choose to call me a child instead of a servant. I thank
you for looking past my blemishes, my sins, and my mistakes and

choosing to lavish your extravagant love on me. Thank you that my identity is not contingent on my actions and that instead it is contingent on your never changing love. Keep me rooted in the perfect love you have for me. I love you, Lord. Amen.

Purpose

*"But you are a chosen people, a royal priesthood, a holy nation,
God's special possession, that you may declare the praises of
him who called you out of darkness into his wonderful light."*
1 Peter 2:9

Sometimes, people limit their opportunities for godly influence because they are too concerned about their success in work, wealth, or knowledge. Pray that your future wife would root herself in her true identity in Christ so that she may carry out her God-given purpose for life.

Lord, thank you for creating each human uniquely, with individual passions, talents, and missions. Thank you for my wife, whom you are working in and through right now. I pray that her identity would remain anchored to the solid foundation of Jesus Christ. Help her to learn more about the ways you designed her and the purpose you have for her life. Let her be reminded that she was created on purpose for a purpose and that you made her for this specific time for a reason. Give her people around her who can sharpen her talents and skills and people who can encourage her to be an active member of the body of Christ. Let her find her value in what you do with her life and not in what she accomplishes. I pray that my purpose unifies strongly with her purpose. Thank you, Lord. Amen.

Thanksgiving

*"I will give thanks to the Lord because of his righteousness;
I will sing the praises of the name of the Lord Most High."*
Psalm 7:17

As you strive to build the habit of gratitude in your life as a single man, pray that you would carry this life-changing habit into your marriage as well.

God, today I ask that my future wife and I would live in a relationship that orbits gratitude. When the storms brew and the clouds are thick, let us cling to the mercies you have shown us. I pray, when we long for the world, when we struggle to have godly motives, and when we covet what belongs to our neighbors, that we might place ourselves in a posture of gratitude. Lord, when the world is against us, let us thank you. When we doubt, let us thank you. When we don't understand what's next, let us thank you. I thank you God for the underserving, vast grace you show us each and every day. You are so good. Amen.

Discipline

"He must be hospitable, one who loves what is good, who is self-controlled, upright, holy and disciplined."
Titus 1:8

Discipline is a trait that is often underestimated. Scripture tells us that as we seek discipline, we gain understanding. Pray that you would integrate necessary disciplines into your life.

Dear God, thank you for the guidance you give me in your word and for providing me with practical wisdom that I can learn from today. I pray that you show me the areas of my life that are undisciplined right now and where I should begin to discipline myself. I pray that I can root myself in a humble posture and not let pride block me from learning the new disciplines you want me to adopt. Let righteous men speak truth, counsel, and direction to me so that you can begin to lead me deeper into sanctification. Show me habits I should integrate into my life, the training I need to go through, and the practices I need to turn from. I trust you Lord, and I am open to your communication of the desires you have for my life. Amen.

Healing

**"Therefore confess your sins to each other and pray
for each other so that you may be healed. The prayer
of a righteous person is powerful and effective."**
James 5:16

**Sin is going to happen in marriage. Make sure you are
turning to God for forgiveness and turning to his people
for healing.**

*God, thank you for the grace you show to your children here on
earth. Thank you for the gift of unity between you and me that
comes through your Son. Thanks for the gift of unity through a marriage I may one day experience in the future. I pray today that my
future wife and I would be honest and transparent with each other
about our struggles and sins. Let no pride or shame hinder us from
confessing our sins to each other out loud. I pray that we would go
to you first for forgiveness and then to each other for healing and
that we would pray for each other. Let our sins only bring us closer
to each other and to you. Let us maintain our unity through hearts
quick to forgive, reflecting the steadfast and never-ending forgiveness
that you show us. Amen.*

Dependency

*"Trust in the Lord with all your heart and lean not
on your own understanding; in all your ways submit
to him, and he will make your paths straight."*
Proverbs 3:5–6

It's natural for people to rely on their own experiences with the world as they make decisions, but with God, they can trust in someone who has gone before them and behind them. Pray that your future wife will be dependent on his will today.

Heavenly Father, today I ask that you would be with my future wife in the decisions she is making, specifically in the small decisions that she faces today. I pray that even if the decisions feel small, she would still strive to include you in them. Father, give her the strength to trust you with her entire heart—not trusting partly in her own abilities and partly in yours. In all her ways, let her not lean not on her own understanding but on your divine wisdom and power. Even if she cannot see above the clouds right now, let her believe—and live out the belief in action—that there is a God watching over her. I love you, Lord. Amen.

Unity

"Therefore if you have any encouragement from being united with Christ, if any comfort from his love, if any common sharing in the Spirit, if any tenderness and compassion, then make my joy complete by being like-minded, having the same love, being one in spirit and of one mind."
Philippians 2:1–2

As you seek to one day become one flesh and live in unity with your wife, remember the gift of the Holy Spirit that you both have been given. Today, ask God to fuse you together in your marriage through the power of his Spirit.

Lord, thank you for the opportunity I have today to bring glory to your name. Today, I pray for unity in my relationship with my future wife. I pray for unity in the greatest sense: through the Holy Spirit. Holy Spirit, I invite you to be the center of our relationship, that you would bind my wife and I together throughout our marriage and that you would govern our minds. I pray that you would walk before us and behind us and through wisdom light the path on which you are leading us. I pray, Holy Spirit, that you would enhance our worship, increase our serving, boost our giving, enrich our relationships, and strengthen our connection with our children. Help us to hear your voice and have open hearts and minds to what you want us to understand. Let us glorify your name. Amen.

Gratitude

"But be sure to fear the Lord and serve him faithfully with all your heart; consider what great things he has done for you."
1 Samuel 12:24

It's easy to focus on what you don't have rather than what God has already given you. Having a heart of gratitude is one of the best ways to find contentment in your life right now. Begin to integrate the habit of gratitude by reflecting on the great things God has done for you.

God, thank you for how you have mysteriously weaved the events of my life together and how I can trust you with what you are doing with my future. Thank you for the ways you have communicated to me, provided for me, and protected me throughout the years. Thank you for calling me your son, allowing me to take part in your story, and using my life as a testament to your grace. I thank you for the relationships I have in my life—the ones I have now and the ones I will have in the future—and the community I have through them. Help me to remember the ways you have brought me through past hardships. I pray that I would turn to you first in all that I do because you are faithful. Thank you for allowing me to pray to you, for listening to my requests, and for being a loving Father who desires a relationship with me. Thank you that your Son is the lead story in my life. I trust you. Amen.

Joyful Sacrifice

"Out of respect for Christ, be courteously reverent to one another."
Ephesians 5:21 (MSG)

Sometimes, you may approach relationships as a duty and not a delight—a project and not a person, a job rather than a joy. Pray that you will be able to joyfully delight in your future wife and that you can serve her continually.

Lord, today I pray that in the relationship I have with my future wife, it would be a delight to serve her rather than a mere duty. Let me not approach this relationship as a bunch of boxes that I need to check but as a relationship I get to be a part of. I pray that I will be eager to treat her well and that I will have a posture of self-sacrifice for her daily. I pray that serving her would not be a duty that I dread nor an obligation that I am constantly frustrated by. Let it not be a job to serve her, but rather a joy. Let there be true joy rooted in you that strengthens the intimacy of our relationship and yields good fruit. Thank you for the blessing she will be in my life. Amen.

Family Reconciliation

"Bear with each other and forgive one another if any of you has a grievance against someone. Forgive as the Lord forgave you. And over all these virtues put on love, which binds them all together in perfect unity."
Colossians 3:13–14

Every family, whether Christian or not, has damaged relationships. Pray that your future wife will begin to work through the pain in her family and be reconciled with those who have offended her.

Lord, thank you for relationships and for designing humans as social creatures with a desire to bond on an intimate level. Thank you for what this reveals about your character. In the fallen world we are in, I know my future wife's family will not be perfect and that there are wounds within her family tree. Lord, you know the depth and complexity of these wounds, and I ask that you would help my wife to begin finding healing from them today. Let her pray the prayers that need to be prayed, repent of the sin she must repent of, confront the people who need to be confronted, and find the reconciliation that you have modeled to us through your Son. Show her where to set boundaries and where to be active. Allow her family to become stronger through unity. Thank you for the power of the forgiveness you showed us, and help us to show that forgiveness to others. Amen.

Search Me

"Search me, God, and know my heart."
Psalm 139:23

King David, a man after God's heart, prayed this prayer, and you can pray it today as well. Be ready for the unexcepted things God might begin to show you.

Father, thank you for the record of men in history who were after your heart. As I seek to desire you more, I come before you now to pray the same prayer David prayed as he sought you. I ask you to search my heart, God. Thoroughly and carefully examine my mind, my will, and my emotions, and know what is inside of me. Father, so often I take my life into my own hands and become the captain of the ship, steering myself to the place I think is best. I ask that you take control and know your son completely. Make your home within my heart. Take inventory of all that is inside of me, and plunge deep into my hurts, struggles, wounds, and pains. Search me and know me, Father. Amen.

Test and Know Me

"Test me and know my anxious thoughts."
Psalm 139:23

God will often call you into tests and trials to burn away the impurities that remain in you. Ask God to test you and discover the anxious thoughts within you.

God, thank you for being close to your children. Continue to press into me and know my heart. As you search me, test me, Father. Just as you tested Noah, Abraham, and your own Son, Jesus, test me too. Allow me to go through heated trials that squeeze out the impurities in me. Let me focus on your protection and faithfulness as you test me and ask me to confront my anxiety and fear. God, find that anxiety and fear that prevent me from living in the freedom you have already afforded me to live in. Thank you for being a God who is always close and who, as you examine my heart and anxious thoughts, chooses to stay close to me and fight with me. Shape me into the person you want me to be by cutting away the sinfulness inside of me.

Notice Offenses

"See if there is any offensive way in me."
Psalm 139:24

As God draws near to you, ask him to reveal to you all the offenses that he finds. Through grace, pray that you might be cleansed of these impurities that you begin to notice.

Dear Father, thank you for revealing yourself to us and making yourself so accessible to us always. I pray to you today and ask that you reveal to me the impurities that bring offense to your name. As you know me, study me, search my heart, test my ways. I ask you boldly to show me these areas of my life that do not line up with whom you are calling me to be. I pray that as you show me these offenses, you would provide for me safe places and faces to help me process these things so that I can find healing in your name. Show me all the ways that offend you and that do not promote love in my life. Give me the grace I need to have with myself as these things surface, and let me receive grace from my peers too. Thank you for being kind enough to indicate the offensives within me. Help me to trust you during this process. Amen.

Resources

As you consider the essential areas of your present and future that you need to pray for, compose a few of your own specific prayers.

_____

_____

_____

_____

_____

_____

_____

_____

_____

_____

_____

_____

_____

_____

_____

_____

_____

_____

If you believe God will one day bless you with the gift of marriage, spend some time crafting a couple of letters to give to your wife one day. These will later serve as powerful reminders of the faithfulness of God and the seeds you planted for your future relationship. There's nothing specific you should write; just write honestly and from your heart. A few things you could write to her about are:

- What God is teaching you right now.
- Commitments you want to make for your future family.
- Where you've seen God's grace recently and how you want to mirror this in your future relationship.
- The specific prayers that you are praying for her.
- Specific struggles and sufferings in your life and how God has pulled you closer to him through these seasons.
- Life lessons that you have recently learned.

Scriptures that Uncover Your Identity

So God created mankind in his own image, in the image of God he created them; male and female he created them.

Genesis 1:27

So in Christ Jesus you are all children of God through faith, for all of you who were baptized into Christ have clothed yourselves with Christ.

Galatians 3:26–27

Do you not know that your bodies are temples of the Holy Spirit, who is in you, whom you have received from God? You are not your own.

1 Corinthians 6:19

Now you are the body of Christ, and each one of you is a part of it.

1 Corinthians 12:27

But the LORD said to Samuel, "Do not consider his appearance or his height, for I have rejected him. The LORD does not look at the things people look at. People look at the outward appearance, but the LORD looks at the heart."

1 Samuel 16:7

But our citizenship is in heaven. And we eagerly await a Savior from there, the Lord Jesus Christ,

Philippians 3:20

Scriptures about Pursuing Holiness

He has saved us and called us to a holy life—not because of anything we have done but because of his own purpose and grace. This grace was given us in Christ Jesus before the beginning of time.

2 Timothy 1:9

How can a young person stay on the path of purity? By living according to your word.

Psalm 119:9

Make every effort to live in peace with everyone and to be holy; without holiness no one will see the Lord.

Hebrews 12:14

Just as you used to offer yourselves as slaves to impurity and to ever-increasing wickedness, so now offer yourselves as slaves to righteousness leading to holiness.

Romans 6:19

Create in me a pure heart, O God, and renew a steadfast spirit within me.

Psalm 51:10

Therefore, since we have these promises, dear friends, let us purify ourselves from everything that contaminates body and spirit, perfecting holiness out of reverence for God.

2 Corinthians 7:1

You were taught, with regard to your former way of life, to put off your old self, which is being corrupted by its deceitful desires; to be made new in the attitude of your minds; and to put on the new self, created to be like God in true righteousness and holiness.

Ephesians 4:22–24

Do not conform to the pattern of this world, but be transformed by the renewing of your mind. Then you will be able to test and approve what God's will is—his good, pleasing and perfect will.

Romans 12:2

Scriptures about Combating Pride

For by the grace given me I say to every one of you: Do not think of yourself more highly than you ought, but rather think of yourself with sober judgment, in accordance with the faith God has distributed to each of you.

Romans 12:3

If anyone thinks they are something when they are not, they deceive themselves.

Galatians 6:3

A fool spurns a parent's discipline, but whoever heeds correction shows prudence.

Proverbs 15:5

All of you, clothe yourselves with humility toward one another, because, "God opposes the proud but shows favor to the humble." Humble yourselves, therefore, under God's mighty hand, that he may lift you up in due time.

1 Peter 5:5–6

For where you have envy and selfish ambition, there you find disorder and every evil practice.

James 3:16

"Whoever does not take up their cross and follow me is not worthy of me."

Matthew 10:38

I have been crucified with Christ and I no longer live, but Christ lives in me. The life I now live in the body, I live by faith in the Son of God, who loved me and gave himself for me.

Galatians 2:20

"Whoever finds their life will lose it, and whoever loses their life for my sake will find it."

Matthew 10:39

Scriptures about Facing Temptations

Fear the LORD your God, serve him only and take your oaths in his name. Do not follow other gods, the gods of the peoples around you;

Deuteronomy 6:13–14

But the Lord is faithful, and he will strengthen you and protect you from the evil one.

2 Thessalonians 3:3

Watch and pray so that you will not fall into temptation. The spirit is willing, but the flesh is weak.

Matthew 26:41

Submit yourselves, then, to God. Resist the devil, and he will flee from you.

James 4:7

No temptation has overtaken you except what is common to mankind. And God is faithful; he will not let you be tempted beyond what you can bear. But when you are tempted, he will also provide a way out so that you can endure it.

1 Corinthians 10:13

Flee the evil desires of youth and pursue righteousness, faith, love and peace, along with those who call on the Lord out of a pure heart.

2 Timothy 2:22

Rather, clothe yourselves with the Lord Jesus Christ, and do not think about how to gratify the desires of the flesh.

Romans 13:14

For the grace of God has appeared that offers salvation to all people. It teaches us to say "No" to ungodliness and worldly passions, and to live self-controlled, upright and godly lives in this present age, while we wait for the blessed hope—the appearing of the glory of our great God and Savior, Jesus Christ, who gave himself for us to redeem us from all wickedness and to purify for himself a people that are his very own, eager to do what is good.

Titus 2:11–14

Scriptures about Finding Freedom from the Past

It is for freedom that Christ has set us free. Stand firm, then, and do not let yourselves be burdened again by a yoke of slavery.

Galatians 5:1

Forget the former things; do not dwell on the past. See, I am doing a new thing! Now it springs up; do you not perceive it? I am making a way in the wilderness and streams in the wasteland.

Isaiah 43:18-19

But one thing I do: Forgetting what is behind and straining toward what is ahead, I press on toward the goal to win the prize for which God has called me heavenward in Christ Jesus.

Philippians 3:13-14

Scriptures about Suffering

Not only so, but we also glory in our sufferings, because we know that suffering produces perseverance; perseverance, character; and character, hope. And hope does not put us to shame, because God's love has been poured out into our hearts through the Holy Spirit, who has been given to us.

Romans 5:3–5

Consider it pure joy, my brothers and sisters, whenever you face trials of many kinds, because you know that the testing of your faith produces perseverance. Let perseverance finish its work so that you may be mature and complete, not lacking anything.

James 1:2–4

I have told you these things, so that in me you may have peace. In this world you will have trouble. But take heart! I have overcome the world.

John 16:33

Therefore, among God's churches we boast about your perseverance and faith in all the persecutions and trials you are enduring. All this is evidence that God's judgment is right, and as a result you will be counted worthy of the kingdom of God, for which you are suffering.

2 Thessalonians 1:4–5

Scriptures about Approaching Grace with Confidence

But God demonstrates his own love for us in this: While we were still sinners, Christ died for us.

Romans 5:8

So if the Son sets you free, you will be free indeed.

John 8:36

He does not treat us as our sins deserve or repay us according to our iniquities.

Psalm 103:10

For I will forgive their wickedness and will remember their sins no more.

Hebrews 8:12

Blessed is the one whose transgressions are forgiven, whose sins are covered. Blessed is the one whose sin the LORD does not count against them and in whose spirit is no deceit.

Psalm 32:1–2

If we confess our sins, he is faithful and just and will forgive us our sins and purify us from all unrighteousness.

1 John 1:9

You are already clean because of the word I have spoken to you.

John 15:3

When you were dead in your sins and in the uncircumcision of your flesh, God made you alive with Christ. He forgave us all our sins, having canceled the charge of our legal indebtedness, which stood against us and condemned us; he has taken it away, nailing it to the cross. And having disarmed the powers and authorities, he made a public spectacle of them, triumphing over them by the cross.

Colossians 2:13–15

The Armor of God

Finally, be strong in the Lord and in his mighty power.
Put on the full armor of God, so that you can take your
stand against the devil's schemes. For our struggle is not
against flesh and blood, but against the rulers, against
the authorities, against the powers of this dark world
and against the spiritual forces of evil in the heavenly
realms. Therefore put on the full armor of God, so that
when the day of evil comes, you may be able to stand
your ground, and after you have done everything, to
stand. Stand firm then, with the belt of truth buckled
around your waist, with the breastplate of righteousness
in place, and with your feet fitted with the readiness
that comes from the gospel of peace. In addition to all
this, take up the shield of faith, with which you can
extinguish all the flaming arrows of the evil one. Take
the helmet of salvation and the sword of the Spirit,
which is the word of God. And pray in the Spirit on all
occasions with all kinds of prayers and requests. With
this in mind, be alert and always keep on praying for all
the Lord's people.

Ephesians 6:10–18

Each one of us engages in a daily battle against evil spiritual
forces of this world. As we remain faithful and allegiant to
God, Satan will constantly target us with attacks, attempt-
ing to derail, discourage, and destroy us. In his letter to the
Ephesians, Paul tells us that we can use God's armor to take

a stand against Satan. Pick up each piece of armor and pray that God will help you put it on so that you can stand firm against Satan's attacks.

The Belt of Truth

Jesus says that Satan's native language is lies (John 8:44). As Satan attacks you with lies, pray that you will remain rooted in God's supreme truth. Pray that you will quickly recognize these lies no matter how truthful they may appear.

The Breastplate of Righteousness

Satan often targets our hearts with his evil plans. Pray that you will pursue holiness and purity in your life daily so that you may guard your heart and not allow Satan any sort of foothold. Pray that you will remain rooted in the extravagant love that God has for you.

The Shoes of the Gospel of Peace

Satan aims to avert our attempts at spreading the gospel around the world. Pray that you will remain motivated, encouraged, eager, and willing to spread the good news of Jesus Christ. Pray that he will keep you focused on the path he wants you to walk.

The Shield of Faith

Our enemy will attack us in clever ways, using the actions and words of others, but nothing can overcome us when God is our protector. Since you can't be certain when Satan will attack you, pray that you will use God's shield to extinguish the flaming arrows he launches at you.

The Helmet of Salvation

Satan will tempt you to doubt your salvation and the promises Jesus has made to you. Pray that your mind may be protected and that you may constantly see the power of Jesus's redemption in new and fresh ways in your life.

The Sword of the Spirit

Sometimes Satan will try to fight you when he's up close and personal. Pray that you will rely on this offensive weapon, the living and active word of God, to counter the snares of Satan. Pray that you will hide God's truth close to your heart and that you will be ready to fight whenever you are attacked.

Connection to God

Praying quick, short prayers throughout the day is a powerful habit to help you win victories over Satan. Pray and make your requests known to God always, and offer yourself in obedience to his Spirit each step of the way.

The Truth about Your Identity

I am a son of God.
Galatians 3:26

I am holy and dearly loved.
Colossians 3:12

I am made in God's image.
Genesis 1:27

I am a citizen of heaven.
Philippians 3:20

I am a part of God's family.
1 Corinthians 12:27

My body is a temple of the Holy Spirit.
1 Corinthians 6:19

I am provided for.
Philippians 4:19

I am a friend of Jesus.
John 15:15

Acknowledgements

This book would not have been possible without the prayers, encouragement, and feedback of so many reverent men and women in my life.

Thank you to my parents, Jeff and Suzanne, for supporting me always. Dad, thank you for constantly pushing me and answering my hundreds of life questions. Thank you, Mom, for always making yourself available, for your kind and joyful heart of service, and for editing many of my writings.

Thank you, Carolyn Fichtner, for teaching me how to pray real prayers anticipating real results and for praying for me constantly. Thank you to Pastor Joey Tvaroch for reading this work and for your encouragement.

Thank you to the group of single men who provided me with open and honest feedback. Mark Gossage and Dalton Williams, I am grateful for the many conversations concerning singleness we have had, and I am blessed by your consistent loyalty in brotherhood. Thank you, Jacob Fierer, for design ideas, for asking the tough questions, and for changing the original title of this book. Andrew Murray, Ben Ellison, and Dalton Odom, this book is better because of your delight in honoring the kingdom through your service to me.